BOOK ANALYSIS

Written by Adriana Carolina Rodríguez Mayo

Translated by Emma Hanna

Wuthering Heights

BY EMILY BRONTË

EMILY BRONTË   9

WUTHERING HEIGHTS   13

SUMMARY   17

The foundling
Changes
Plotting revenge
A matter of inheritance
Back to the present

CHARACTER STUDY   27

Heathcliff
Catherine Earnshaw
Edgar Linton
Hindley Earnshaw
Isabella Linton
Ellen "Nelly" Dean
Lockwood
Hareton Earnshaw
Linton Heathcliff
Cathy Linton

ANALYSIS   35

Form
Themes

FURTHER REFLECTION   49

FURTHER READING   53

EMILY BRONTË

ENGLISH NOVELIST AND POET

- **Born in Yorkshire in 1818.**
- **Died in Yorkshire in 1848.**
- **Notable works:**
  - *Wuthering Heights* (1847), novel
  - *Poems by Currer, Ellis and Acton Bell* (1846), poetry anthology (published jointly with her sisters Anne and Charlotte under male pseudonyms)

Emily Brontë is one of the most famous English writers of the 19th century, but very little is known about her personal life. All surviving accounts of her life are shrouded in a certain degree of mystery and contain a number of gaps, as she led a somewhat solitary life as a result of her innate shyness and reclusive tendencies. Her mother and two of her older sisters died when she was very young, and since the cause of their sisters' deaths was tuberculosis, which they had contracted at school, Emily and her other siblings were withdrawn from school and educated at home for the rest of their youth.

The Brontë home was an isolated, lonely house, and the siblings had almost no contact with anyone other than their father and aunt. This meant that they had to learn to entertain themselves, and they spent most of their time making up and writing stories about imaginary kingdoms. A number of these manuscripts have survived to the present day, and are considered the forerunners of the literary style that would come to characterise the three sisters' later works, as Anne and Charlotte Brontë also went on to become famous writers, with the latter's novel *Jane Eyre* (1847) being particularly successful.

Emily died of tuberculosis at the age of 30. Today, very little is known about her aside from what her older sister Charlotte wrote about her.

DID YOU KNOW?

Emily and her sisters initially had to publish their works under male pseudonyms, because in those days writing was not seen as a typical or appropriate profession for a woman. *Wuthering Heights* was therefore initially published under the name Ellis Bell.

WUTHERING HEIGHTS

STAR-CROSSED LOVE ON THE RUGGED MOORS

- **Genre:** realist novel/Romantic novel
- **Reference edition:** Brontë, E. (1992) *Wuthering Heights*. Ware: Wordsworth.
- **1st edition:** 1847
- **Themes:** symbolism, tempestuous relationships, duality

Wuthering Heights tells the story of two individuals whose love for each other is doomed to end in tragedy because of circumstances beyond their control. The story begins when a young man called Lockwood, who has rented out a house called Thrushcross Grange, goes to visit his landlord Heathcliff, who lives nearby in a place called Wuthering Heights. Heathcliff's extremely guarded demeanour awakens Lockwood's curiosity, and he becomes fascinated by this wild, uncouth, mysterious man. He then asks his housekeeper, Ellen Dean, what she knows about Heathcliff; it is a subject she knows well, and she begins to recount everything she knows about Heathcliff's relationship with the Earnshaws and the Lintons, the two families who used to own Thrushcross Grange and Wuthering Heights.

SUMMARY

THE FOUNDLING

One day, Mr Earnshaw, the owner of Wuthering Heights, brings home a young dark-skinned boy called Heathcliff. Mr Earnshaw has adopted him, and intends to raise him alongside his other two children, Hindley and Catherine. Initially, these blonde-haired, pale-skinned siblings do not take kindly to the intruder in their midst, but Catherine eventually mellows towards him.

Even after Heathcliff and Catherine become friends, Hindley – the elder of the two – never accepts his adopted brother, and constantly mocks his appearance, origins and half-feral behaviour. Heathcliff endures Hindley's bullying as best he can, and seeks solace in his blossoming friendship with Catherine. They spend most of their childhood together, and forge an extremely strong bond which only deepens when Hindley leaves for university, leaving the two younger children free to spend their time together without a care in the world.

However, this tranquillity is shattered when Mr Earnshaw dies and Hindley, who has now graduated from university, returns to Wuthering Heights. He has married a woman called Frances, and all he wants is to claim his place as the rightful lord and master of his ancestral home.

Hindley only permits Heathcliff to remain at Wuthering Heights as a servant, and continues mistreating him as the years go by. Furthermore, Hindley's behaviour towards Catherine is nothing short of tyrannical, which the young woman finds unbearable; as a result, she is increasingly drawn to Heathcliff, whom she sees as an ally.

CHANGES

One night, Catherine and Heathcliff decide to go to Thrushcross Grange to spy on Edgar and Isabella Linton, two spoiled, wealthy children who live there. When they are trying to leave, Catherine is bitten by a dog and is forced to stay with the Lintons at Thrushcross Grange to recuperate, while Heathcliff is sent back to Wuthering Heights.

While Heathcliff is left feeling bereft without Catherine by his side, the Lintons grow fond of her, particularly Edgar, who believes that she is letting her potential go to waste. He therefore decides to transform her from a wild, impulsive girl into a demure, elegant young lady. Heathcliff barely recognises her when she returns to Wuthering Heights, and this new Catherine feels like a stranger to him.

Meanwhile, Frances has a son called Hareton, but dies in childbirth. Hindley never bonds with his son, whom he sees as a weakling, and descends into alcoholism. He also becomes even more aggressive towards Heathcliff as an outlet for all his rage and frustration now that his wife is no longer around to temper his violent outbursts. He becomes so volatile that his abuse and alcoholism begin to affect everyone at the house.

Catherine realises that Edgar Linton has fallen in love with her, but she confides in her housekeeper that even though she is not as close to Heathcliff as she once was, her heart belongs to him. However, she also acknowledges that she could not make a life with him without lowering her station, which is the only part of the conversation Heathcliff overhears. He is deeply wounded, and decides to leave Wuthering Heights.

PLOTTING REVENGE

Heathcliff does not come back for another three years, which he spends making his fortune through shady business deals. Separated from her true love, Catherine decides to marry Edgar Linton and moves to Thrushcross Grange.

Heathcliff returns to Wuthering Heights, bolstered by his newfound wealth but consumed by resentment and driven by his determination to achieve one particular goal: the complete destruction of Hindley, whose alcoholism has left him in an utterly wretched state. He plans to trick Hindley into racking up major gambling debts so that he has no choice but to mortgage the property he inherited from his father, meaning that Heathcliff will be able to purchase it at a much lower price and take everything from his greatest enemy. However, he is not satisfied to simply ruin the eldest Earnshaw's life – he also wants to take revenge on Edgar Linton by acquiring Thrushcross Grange.

Once his plan has been put into action, Heathcliff reveals a different side of his personality: a crueller, darker persona that has no qualms about trampling over anyone who stands in the way of him pursuing his goals. Before long, he is successful: Hindley loses Wuthering Heights, and Heathcliff buys it. He also pays frequent visits to Catherine at Thrushcross Grange, but Edgar treats him like a pariah and makes it clear that he is not welcome there. Heathcliff therefore decides to take his revenge on Edgar by seducing Isabella Linton, and he eventually marries her, even though he secretly despises her, as this is the only way he will be able to get his hands on the Linton property.

After Heathcliff and Isabella's wedding, the animosity between him and Edgar reaches boiling point, which leaves Catherine so distressed that she falls ill.

Catherine's health deteriorates further, and the housekeeper Ellen arranges for Heathcliff to visit her in secret one last time; just hours later, she dies giving birth to a daughter. Edgar names the child Cathy, after her mother, and raises her in total ignorance of the existence of Wuthering Heights and its owner.

Meanwhile, Hindley's alcoholism leads him into an early grave, and Heathcliff becomes his son Hareton's guardian and the legal owner of Wuthering Heights. As vengeance for all the humiliation he suffered at Hindley's hands, Heathcliff refuses to let Hareton be educated and treats him like a servant.

The death of Catherine has left Isabella feeling miserable, and she is no longer able to endure Heathcliff's volatile temper and lack of affection towards her. She leaves for London, where she gives birth to a sickly son called Linton.

A MATTER OF INHERITANCE

Edgar manages to keep Cathy confined to Thrushcross Grange for 13 years, but the young girl is very curious about the surrounding area, and has a strong desire to explore the moors around her home. One day, she manages to slip out and ends up at Wuthering Heights, where she meets Hareton; however, she considers him uncouth and uncivilised. Edgar forces her to return to the grange and warns her not to leave the house without his permission again.

When Isabella dies, Edgar takes charge of his nephew Linton and brings him to live at Thrushcross Grange. However, Heathcliff insists that, as his father, he should have custody of the boy instead, even though his son has never met him.

One day, Cathy meets Linton and starts exchanging love letters with him. When Heathcliff learns of this situation, he encourages the budding romance between them and goes behind Edgar's back to help them get to know each other better. One day, he invites Cathy to Wuthering Heights and coerces her into marrying Linton in order to strengthen his own claim to Thrushcross Grange.

Edgar and Linton both die shortly afterwards, and Heathcliff forces Cathy to move to Wuthering Heights to work for him. This allows him to become the legal owner of Thrushcross Grange.

BACK TO THE PRESENT

After listening to the entire story, as told to him by the housekeeper Ellen Dean, Lockwood is too repulsed by everything that has happened at Thrushcross Grange to continue living there, and he decides to return to the city.

However, Lockwood eventually returns to Wuthering Heights, where he witnesses the first stirrings of friendship springing up between Cathy and Hareton, the son of Hindley and Frances. Cathy starts teaching him how to read, and they gradually fell in love and decide to marry. Heathcliff is so consumed by his rage, sorrow and desperate longing to be reunited with his beloved Catherine that he does not even notice the romance that is kindling between the two young people right under his nose, and dies alone, with only Catherine's ghost for company.

INSPIRATION CLOSE TO HOME

While she was writing part of her novel, Emily Brontë also spent a great deal of her time looking after her brother Branwell, who suffered from alcoholism and eventually died from it. This has led a number of critics to speculate that some of the characters' personality traits were inspired by his erratic behaviour.

CHARACTER STUDY

The name of the novel echoes a number of the characters' personalities, as the words "wuthering heights" call to mind a very specific type of imagery: wild, rugged terrain, windswept moors and bleak, rainy days. Furthermore, Brontë's characters are contradictory and enigmatic, and often vacillate between wild impulsiveness and cold, calculating logic.

HEATHCLIFF

Heathcliff has a dark complexion, dark eyes and black, curly hair. Although his adoptive father loves him immediately, his adoptive brother rejects him because of his physical appearance, and the rest of the family are suspicious of him because of his origins and because he looks different to them.

His personality is complex and contradictory; although he sometimes lets himself be controlled by the intensity of his emotions, he can also act in a cold, calculating manner and devise elaborate, strategic plans in order to further his ambitions. The hardships he endures have a lasting impact on him, transforming him from a sensitive boy to an indolent, greedy, calculating, cruel man.

He is never able to be with Catherine, the love of his life, and her death plunges him even further into the depths of bitterness and despair. His weariness and pain drive him to ruin the lives of everyone around him. Catherine is very well acquainted with his dark side and bad intentions:

> "Nelly, help me to convince her of her madness. Tell her what Heathcliff is: an unreclaimed creature, without refinement, without cultivation: an arid wilderness of furze and whinstone. I'd as soon put that little canary into the park on a winter's day, as recommend you to bestow your heart on him! It is deplorable ignorance of his character, child, and nothing else, which makes that dream enter your head. Pray, don't imagine that he conceals depths of benevolence and affection beneath a stern exterior!" (p. 74)

CATHERINE EARNSHAW

Catherine is a blonde, fair-skinned girl who grows into a beautiful woman. She is somewhat arrogant and initially distrusts the young boy her father brings home, but she later comes to consider him her closest friend and confidant.

She is also rather spoiled, capricious and shallow, and she cares deeply about what other people think of her. She always seems to be full of energy, at least until she falls ill, and has a knack for extracting herself from difficult situations with grace and poise.

Heathcliff is the love of her life, but she marries Edgar Linton because of her pride, spitefulness and fear of losing her social status.

EDGAR LINTON

Edgar is the heir to Thrushcross Grange. He is a well-educated, aristocratic young man who is deeply in love with Catherine. He has a daughter with her and treats her very tenderly, but he dislikes Heathcliff, in no small part because he believes that his relationship with his wife is inappropriate.

He loves his daughter and wants the best for her, but this drives him to become very overprotective of her. He holds both others and himself to extremely high standards.

HINDLEY EARNSHAW

Hindley is Catherine's older brother, and is an insensitive, cruel man. He hates Heathcliff because he is jealous of the affection shown to him by his father, and treats him very badly. This shows that he is a tyrant who utterly lacks compassion and who enjoys humiliating people who are weaker than him.

After the death of his wife, he becomes even more bad-tempered and squanders all his money on alcohol and gambling. He drives all the other characters away with his selfishness and abusiveness, and dies alone.

ISABELLA LINTON

Isabella is Edgar's sister and later marries Heathcliff. She is a reserved, well-mannered woman and a submissive wife who is incapable of standing up to her husband's aggression, and eventually runs away from him while she is pregnant with their son. Like Catherine, she is rather wilful and capricious, which leads her to marry her brother's greatest enemy despite him warning her against the match.

ELLEN "NELLY" DEAN

When Lockwood arrives at Thrushcross Grange, Ellen is the person who tells him the whole story about his new lodgings. She is a caring, affectionate woman who grew up with Catherine, Heathcliff and Hindley, and later becomes the housekeeper of Thrushcross Grange. She also displays great sensitivity and is very understanding.

LOCKWOOD

Lockwood is the new tenant at Thrushcross Grange. He is an observant young man with a curious mind who describes himself as an introvert, and initially believes that he has found a kind of kindred spirit in Heathcliff's reserved, unfriendly nature. However, he is disgusted by his landlord after hearing his full story.

HARETON EARNSHAW

Hareton is Hindley's son. He is raised by Heathcliff, who denies the boy an education as revenge for the mistreatment he suffered at the hands of his father, and his time in Heathcliff's custody transforms him into a gruff, bad-tempered man.

LINTON HEATHCLIFF

Heathcliff's son is a sickly child who is very easy to manipulate. He is obedient and knows nothing about his family, which his father uses to his advantage in order to exact his revenge on Edgar. Linton marries Cathy, but their marriage is cut short when he dies soon afterwards.

CATHY LINTON

Cathy is an impulsive, rather rebellious young woman who gets sucked into Heathcliff's plan to seize Thrushcross Hall. As part of this plan, she is coerced into marrying Heathcliff's son Linton. Like her mother Catherine, she is strong-willed, daring and tenacious, which leads her to spend some time working for Heathcliff as a servant after her husband's death. During this time, she gets to know Hareton Earnshaw, and their eventual marriage means that they become joint heirs to both Wuthering Heights and Thrushcross Grange.

ANALYSIS

FORM

Genre

A Romantic novel?

Wuthering Heights was met with a mixed critical reception when it was first published, partly because of its unusual form, which resisted simple classification according to the genre conventions of the time. Even today, identifying a single genre that comprehensively defines the novel is no easy matter.

Romanticism is a literary genre which emerged in Germany and England in the early 19th century. The genre's defining traits include the predominance of emotion over reason and the glorification of individualism; many Romantic works are therefore centred on a protagonist who tends to experience strong emotions.

Although *Wuthering Heights* also contains elements which are not generally associated with Romantic literature, the characters' turbulent emotions and the way their moods and personalities are mirrored by their wild surroundings and the stormy weather are certainly characteristic of Romanticism. In fact, it seems as though every element of the novel is affected by the characters and their state of mind: for example, storms blow up every time something extremely shocking happens or when something goes wrong, and the houses seem to be falling into disrepair in tandem with Heathcliff's downward spiral.

Another characteristic of Romantic fiction is its fascination with otherness. In this novel, this idea is explored through the character of Heathcliff, who is in constant conflict with the rest of the family because he comes from a different social and ethnic background. In fact, he is frequently described as "half-wild", and therefore fundamentally different from the rest of the Earnshaws. In fact, it could even be said that from Hindley's perspective, his fears are eventually proven well-founded, as Heathcliff eventually turns violent and destroys the family from within (although it is also worth noting that it is Hindley's mistreatment that drives him to do so).

The novel also incorporates a supernatural element, as Heathcliff and a number of the other characters see Catherine's ghost after her death. However, this is left ambiguous, and the reader can choose to interpret her appearance as a genuine haunting or simply as a product of the other characters' imaginations due to their obsessive recurring thoughts about her.

A realist novel?

Wuthering Heights could also be described as a realist novel, given that it provides a realistic depiction of rural life in 19th-century England. Realism is a literary movement which emerged in the second half of the 19th century, and is often seen as both a rejection of and an alternative to the Romantic aesthetics that had dominated art and literature during the first half of the century.

The novel's accurate descriptions of the settings, characters, behaviours and events it portrays allow modern readers to better understand what that era was like. For example, it is made clear that Heathcliff's social and ethnic background – Lockwood describes him as "a dark-skinned gypsy in aspect" (p. 3) – was considered out of place in a well-off family at that time. We are also shown that it was much more difficult to end a marriage, as Isabella is forced to endure Heathcliff's abuse and surliness for a considerable amount of time because divorcing him was not an option. They remain legally married even after she leaves him, which Heathcliff uses to his advantage in order to seize her inheritance.

Structure

The novel's structure employs a frame story, which is a narrative device whereby the main story is "nested" within another, broader narrative.

In this case, the frame story involves Mr Lockwood asking his housekeeper to tell him about his landlord Heathcliff. The novel then jumps back in time and recounts Heathcliff's story from the beginning, temporarily abandoning the narrative thread which focused on Lockwood.

This nested narrative follows Heathcliff through his childhood and adolescence at Wuthering Heights, and explores his turbulent relationships with Catherine and her brother Hindley. As the story progresses, the events it describes become more recent; the focus shifts to the second generations of the families that own the two properties, until the narrative eventually catches up to the present and returns to Lockwood's story.

However, there are also a number of interruptions throughout the book when the narrative suddenly jumps back to the present while the housekeeper is telling Lockwood this story. This is often because Lockwood is so overwhelmed or shocked by the story that he requests a break from hearing it, during which he muses on everything he has discovered. Lockwood also acts as a witness to the disastrous results of his landlord's unquenchable thirst for vengeance, and allows the reader to see how Heathcliff has been reduced to a wretched, miserable soul who has lost everything he cared about most.

Finally, the novel also flashes forward into the future: as we have already mentioned in the summary, Lockwood decides to return to London after learning what his landlord is really like and what he has done. At this point, the novel refocuses on the second generation of characters, whose story then intersects with Lockwood's: he returns to Thrushcross Grange, and discovers that the past is finally relinquishing its grip on the two houses, as all the resentment, pain and desire for revenge that had hung over them like a shroud are dispelled with Heathcliff's death. Instead, new love is blossoming, and the next generation are breaking free of the vicious cycle created by their fathers' mistakes and are forging a more hopeful future together.

This non-linear timeline also allows important information to be hidden in plain sight – in the first chapters of the novel, when Lockwood visits Heathcliff, there are a number of characters in the background of the scene who are very easy to overlook and seem unimportant at first glance. However, by the time the novel definitively returns to Lockwood's perspective as the story is drawing to a close, we have discovered a great deal about these deceptively important characters, and they play a key role in the novel's conclusion.

THEMES

Symbolism

Wuthering Heights is full of objects and phenomena which are imbued with multiple meanings. For example, Lockwood has nightmares when he sleeps in the bed Catherine died in, and it is later revealed that this bed is not only where she breathed her last, but was also where she sought refuge from her brother's tyranny. Heathcliff eventually dies in the same bed following several days of delirium, which could be interpreted as a metaphor for the way their love was unconsummated in life but is strong enough to unite them in death.

The theme of illness is more than just a narrative device, and plays an extremely important role in the novel: it is used to deepen our understanding of a number of scenes and characters, and leads to many important revelations. For example, if we examine the way Catherine's health deteriorates during her marriage to Edgar, it becomes clear that this decline reflects her crumbling relationship with Heathcliff, who has made it his life's mission to destroy her and Edgar's lives.

When she falls pregnant with Edgar's child the rift between her and Heathcliff widens further, and they are never more distant than when she goes into labour; accordingly, she dies during childbirth. Her daughter Cathy could be viewed as the symbol of Catherine's own spirit, cast out of her body by her despair at the realisation that she will never be united with her true love.

Finally, the houses themselves are drenched in symbolism, and are frequently presented as opposites. While Thrushcross Grange is always described as peaceful, homely and welcoming, Wuthering Heights is described as a place which is hard to reach, inhospitable and falling into disrepair. Both properties are a reflection of their respective owners, and when Heathcliff eventually lays claim to Thrushcross Grange, its former splendour seems to diminish. In the end, both properties mirror Heathcliff's own decline and his disregard for both his own life and the lives of others.

Tempestuous relationships

The novel depicts a number of tempestuous relationships, including Heathcliff's stormy relationship with his adoptive brother Hindley and Hindley's relationship with his father. Hindley's issues with Heathcliff stem from the fact that Hindley does not understand why his father wants to bring another boy into their home, and views Heathcliff as a rival for his father's affections.

Of course, the stormiest relationship depicted in the novel is the star-crossed love between Catherine and Heathcliff, who love and hurt each other in equal measure, and allow their pride and stubbornness to drive them apart. The special connection that binds them together also gives them a profound understanding of each other's weak spots:

> "My love for Linton is like the foliage in the woods: time will change it, I'm well aware, as winter changes the trees. My love for Heathcliff resembles the eternal rocks beneath: a source of little visible delight, but necessary. Nelly, I am Heathcliff! He's always, always in my mind: not as a pleasure, any more than I am always a pleasure to myself, but as my own being." (p. 59)

The novel therefore features a number of twists and turns: at certain times, we are led to believe that Heathcliff and Catherine's love story will have a happy ending, that they will declare their love for each other and build a life together, while at other moments we start to doubt that their feelings for each other are genuine and wonder if they would both be better off apart. This constant shift between an exploration of a profound, tender romance and drama that borders on tragedy means that the novel cannot necessarily be labelled a love story.

Many of the greatest disasters which occur in the novel, such as the collapse of Heathcliff and Isabella's marriage, are precipitated by fights between Heathcliff and Catherine. The relationship between Isabella and Heathcliff is another example of tempestuous love, as Isabella's flights of fancy lead her to marry Heathcliff despite her brother's opposition to the match. In fact, their marriage is downright unhealthy, as Isabella puts up with Heathcliff's abuse and indifference towards her for a long time.

Edgar and Catherine do love each other in their own way, although Heathcliff always casts a long shadow over their relationship. Their relationship seems much more stable than most of the others in the novel, as they are opposites who complement each other. However, appearances can be deceiving, and deep down Catherine has never forgotten about her first love; her distress over the constant fights and arguments between Heathcliff and her husband even cause her death.

Cathy and Linton find themselves trapped in an arranged marriage devised by Heathcliff as a means of getting his hands on Thrushcross Grange. Their marriage makes life more difficult for both of them, although Cathy is soon widowed when her sickly young husband finally succumbs to one of his illnesses.

The only love story in the novel which does not end in tragedy is the last one to be introduced, namely the romance between Cathy and Hareton. Their stable, healthy relationship has a happy ending and finally brings peace to both houses.

Duality

The novel is full of opposing elements which attract and repel each other. The characters have strong, stubborn, passionate personalities, and love and hate with equal intensity.

Heathcliff and Hindley are originally portrayed as total opposites. However, as we progress through the novel, we see that Heathcliff meets the same end as Hindley by becoming an alcoholic tyrant, and both men's degeneration into gruff, reclusive individuals who mistreat everyone around them is triggered by the pain of losing the woman they love.

Hareton also mirrors many of Heathcliff's characteristics: they are both young men without a family, whose origins result in them being treated as outcasts at Wuthering Heights. Furthermore, neither of them received an education in their youth, and they have very bad manners, but are noble at heart in spite of their uncouth nature.

Meanwhile, Isabella and Catherine are also presented as opposites: Isabella is a submissive wife who is incapable of standing up to Heathcliff and challenging him, whereas Catherine's interactions with Heathcliff are unpredictable, as she is not afraid of him and treats him as an equal or even acts arrogantly towards him. Cathy, like her mother, is impulsive, stubborn and ill-mannered, so when she eventually marries Hareton, their relationship almost seems to mirror the first romance which flourished between two people from these opposite worlds.

FURTHER REFLECTION

SOME QUESTIONS TO THINK ABOUT...

- What aspects of *Wuthering Heights* could be considered symbolic?
- How does the novel reflect 19th-century English society?
- The novel's two protagonists are never able to be together. Why is this important, and why is this outcome made apparent to the reader before the end of the novel? Explain your answer.
- Why is it significant that *Wuthering Heights* was written by a woman?
- Why do you think the author used parallels and contrasts between the characters to create a sense of duality at various points in the novel? Explain your answer.
- What role do servants play in *Wuthering Heights*? In your answer, pay particular attention to the fact that the main story is narrated by the housekeeper.

We want to hear from you!
Leave a comment on your online library
and share your favourite books on social media!

FURTHER READING

REFERENCE EDITION

- Brontë, E. (1992) *Wuthering Heights*. Ware: Wordsworth.

REFERENCE STUDIES

- Bump, J. (1997) La teoría de los sistemas familiares, la adicción y *Cumbres borrascosas*. *Style*. 31(2), pp. 328-350.

- Levin, N. (2012) "I am Heathcliff!" Paradoxical love in Bronte's *Wuthering Heights. University of Stockholm*. [Online]. [Accessed 6 April 2018]. Available from: <http://www.diva-portal.org/smash/get/diva2:538526/fulltext01.pdf>

RECOMMENDED READING

- Oates, J. C. (1982) The magnanimity of *Wuthering Heights. Critical Inquiry*. Vol. 9(2), pp. 435-449.

ADAPTATIONS

- *Wuthering Heights*. (1939) [Film]. William Wyler. Dir. USA: Samuel Goldwyn Productions.

- *Wuthering Heights*. (2009) [TV series]. Coky Giedroyc. Dir. UK: ITV.

- *Wuthering Heights*. (2011) [Film]. Andrea Arnold. Dir. UK: HanWay Film.

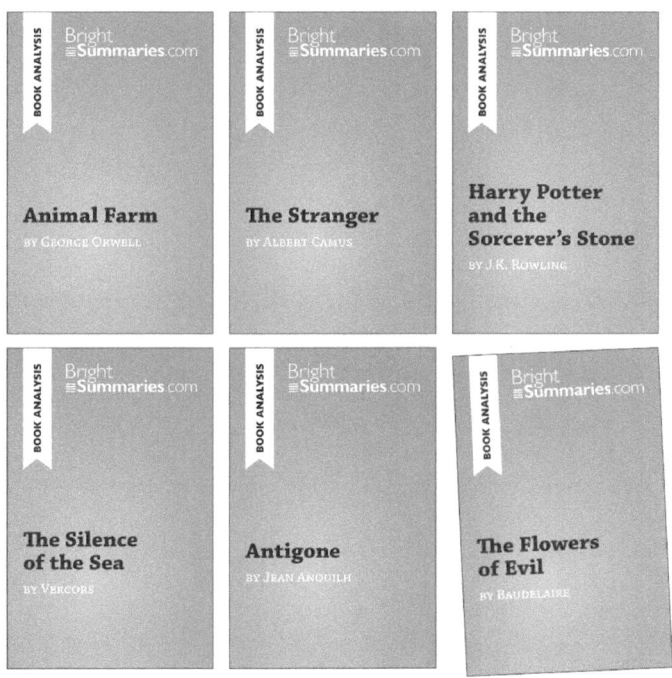

www.brightsummaries.com

Ebook EAN: 9782808001885

Paperback EAN: 9782808001892

Legal Deposit: D/2017/12603/615

Cover: © Primento

Digital conception by Primento, the digital partner of
publishers.